MAD LIBS

75th ANNIVERSARY

The WIZARD of OZ

concept created by Roger Price & Leonard Stern

PSS!

P9-BZU-028

PRICE STERN SLOAN

An Imprint of Penguin Group (USA)

PRICE STERN SLOAN
Published by the Penguin Group
Penguin Group (USA), 375 Hudson Street, New York, New York 10014, USA

USA | Canada | UK | Ireland | Australia | New Zealand | India | South Africa | China
Penguin Books Ltd, Registered Offices: 80 Strand, London WC2R 0RL, England

For more information about the Penguin Group visit penguin.com

Published by Price Stern Sloan,
a division of Penguin Young Readers Group,
345 Hudson Street, New York, New York 10014.

ISBN 978-0-8431-8017-6

3 5 7 9 10 8 6 4 2

ALWAYS LEARNING   PEARSON

MAD LIBS
INSTRUCTIONS

MAD LIBS® is a game for people who don't like games! It can be played by one, two, three, four, or forty.

• RIDICULOUSLY SIMPLE DIRECTIONS

In this tablet you will find stories containing blank spaces where words are left out. One player, the READER, selects one of these stories. The READER does not tell anyone what the story is about. Instead, he/she asks the other players, the WRITERS, to give him/her words. These words are used to fill in the blank spaces in the story.

• TO PLAY

The READER asks each WRITER in turn to call out a word—an adjective or a noun or whatever the space calls for—and uses them to fill in the blank spaces in the story. The result is a MAD LIBS® game.

When the READER then reads the completed MAD LIBS® game to the other players, they will discover that they have written a story that is fantastic, screamingly funny, shocking, silly, crazy, or just plain dumb—depending upon which words each WRITER called out.

• EXAMPLE (*Before* and *After*)

"_____!" he said _____
EXCLAMATION   ADVERB

as he jumped into his convertible _____ and
                                         NOUN

drove off with his _____ wife.
                        ADJECTIVE

"_____*Ouch*_____!" he said _____*stupidly*_____
EXCLAMATION   ADVERB

as he jumped into his convertible _____*cat*_____ and
                                         NOUN

drove off with his _____*brave*_____ wife.
                        ADJECTIVE

In case you have forgotten what adjectives, adverbs, nouns, and verbs are, here is a quick review:

An ADJECTIVE describes something or somebody. *Lumpy, soft, ugly, messy,* and *short* are adjectives.

An ADVERB tells how something is done. It modifies a verb and usually ends in "ly." *Modestly, stupidly, greedily,* and *carefully* are adverbs.

A NOUN is the name of a person, place, or thing. *Sidewalk, umbrella, bridle, bathtub,* and *nose* are nouns.

A VERB is an action word. *Run, pitch, jump,* and *swim* are verbs. Put the verbs in past tense if the directions say PAST TENSE. *Ran, pitched, jumped,* and *swam* are verbs in the past tense.

When we ask for A PLACE, we mean any sort of place: a country or city (*Spain, Cleveland*) or a room (*bathroom, kitchen*).

An EXCLAMATION or SILLY WORD is any sort of funny sound, gasp, grunt, or outcry, like *Wow!, Ouch!, Whomp!, Ick!,* and *Gadzooks!*

When we ask for specific words, like a NUMBER, a COLOR, an ANIMAL, or a PART OF THE BODY, we mean a word that is one of those things, like *seven, blue, horse,* or *head*.

When we ask for a PLURAL, it means more than one. For example, *cat* pluralized is *cats*.

MAD LIBS® is fun to play with friends, but you can also play it by yourself! To begin with, DO NOT look at the story on the page below. Fill in the blanks on this page with the words called for. Then, using the words you have selected, fill in the blank spaces in the story.

Now you've created your own hilarious MAD LIBS® game!

WE'RE OFF TO SEE THE WIZARD

ADJECTIVE _____

ADVERB _____

PERSON IN ROOM (MALE) _____

PERSON IN ROOM (FEMALE) _____

ANIMAL _____

ADJECTIVE _____

NOUN _____

NOUN _____

ADJECTIVE _____

NUMBER _____

NOUN _____

ADJECTIVE _____

NOUN _____

NOUN _____

PLURAL NOUN _____

TYPE OF FOOD _____

NOUN _____

SAME NOUN _____

MAD☺LIBS®

OZ IN MODERN TIMES

Imagine how different *The Wizard of Oz* would be in today's world:

- Dorothy could update her status on _____-book,
  PART OF THE BODY

  letting her _____ back in (the) _____
  PLURAL NOUN   A PLACE

  know she was safe in Oz.

- The Tin Man could buy a/an _____ on
  PART OF THE BODY

  _____-bay.
  LETTER OF THE ALPHABET

- The _____ Witch of the West could track Dorothy
  ADJECTIVE

  by following her Insta-_____ account.
  NOUN

- The Scarecrow could take online classes at _____
  NOUN

  University to earn his _____.
  NOUN

- The _____ of Oz could talk to his _____
  NOUN   PLURAL NOUN

  on Skype instead of in person.

- The Munchkins could earn $_____ by bringing their
  NUMBER

  _____ act to Broadway.
  ADJECTIVE

- And Dorothy could hitch a ride back to (the) _____
  A PLACE

  on a/an _____ 747 jumbo _____.
  ADJECTIVE   NOUN

MAD LIBS® is fun to play with friends, but you can also play it by yourself! To begin with, DO NOT look at the story on the page below. Fill in the blanks on this page with the words called for. Then, using the words you have selected, fill in the blank spaces in the story.

Now you've created your own hilarious MAD LIBS® game!

BOOK IT

NOUN _____

VERB _____

ADJECTIVE _____

NOUN _____

ADJECTIVE _____

COLOR _____

NOUN _____

ADVERB _____

PLURAL NOUN _____

ADJECTIVE _____

ADJECTIVE _____

ADVERB _____

NOUN _____

COLOR _____

PLURAL NOUN _____

ARTICLE OF CLOTHING (PLURAL) _____

VERB (PAST TENSE) _____

COLOR _____

MAD LIBS

BOOK IT

Many people don't know that *The* _____ *of Oz* is actually
NOUN

based on a book! Just in case you don't have the time to

_____ it, here are a few _____ things to
VERB   ADJECTIVE

know about the _____ that inspired your favorite movie.
NOUN

In the book, the Land of Oz is a/an _____ place and not just
ADJECTIVE

a dream. And Dorothy's _____ slippers are actually silver!
COLOR

In the movie, Dorothy is shown as a/an _____ in distress.
NOUN

But in the book, she is _____ the one who saves her
ADVERB

_____ from _____ trouble! The _____
PLURAL NOUN   ADJECTIVE   ADJECTIVE

Witch of the West is _____ evil in the movie, but she plays a
ADVERB

much smaller _____ in the book. And in the book, before
NOUN

entering the _____ City, Dorothy and her _____
COLOR   PLURAL NOUN

were required to wear green _____. In the
ARTICLE OF CLOTHING (PLURAL)

movie, they just _____ right in, and everything was
VERB (PAST TENSE)

_____!
COLOR

MAD LIBS® is fun to play with friends, but you can also play it by yourself! To begin with, DO NOT look at the story on the page below. Fill in the blanks on this page with the words called for. Then, using the words you have selected, fill in the blank spaces in the story.

Now you've created your own hilarious MAD LIBS® game!

FAMOUS LINES

EXCLAMATION _____

NUMBER _____

NOUN _____

ADJECTIVE _____

A PLACE _____

SAME PLACE _____

ANIMAL (PLURAL) _____

EXCLAMATION _____

ADJECTIVE _____

ANIMAL _____

VERB _____

NOUN _____

VERB ENDING IN "ING" _____

SAME VERB ENDING IN "ING" _____

NOUN _____

NOUN _____

PERSON IN ROOM _____

A PLACE _____

MAD LIBS
FAMOUS LINES

_____! There are at least _____ famous lines from *The*
  EXCLAMATION   NUMBER

_____ *of Oz* that are still well-known today. Which one do
  NOUN

you think is the most _____?
           ADJECTIVE

- "There's no place like (the) _____. There's no
                  A PLACE

  place like (the) _____."
              SAME PLACE

- "_____ and tigers and bears, _____!"
  ANIMAL (PLURAL)   EXCLAMATION

- "I'll get you, my _____, and your little
               ADJECTIVE

  _____, too!"
  ANIMAL

- "_____ no attention to that man behind the
    VERB

  _____!"
  NOUN

- "I'm _____! _____! Oh,
    VERB ENDING IN "ING"   SAME VERB ENDING IN "ING"

  what a/an _____! What a/an _____!"
         NOUN   NOUN

- "_____, I've a feeling we're not in (the)
  PERSON IN ROOM

  _____ anymore."
  A PLACE

Published by Price Stern Sloan, an imprint of Penguin Group (USA), 345 Hudson Street, New York, NY 10014.

MAD LIBS® is fun to play with friends, but you can also play it by yourself! To begin with, DO NOT look at the story on the page below. Fill in the blanks on this page with the words called for. Then, using the words you have selected, fill in the blank spaces in the story.

Now you've created your own hilarious MAD LIBS® game!

RUBY SLIPPERS

COLOR _____

ADJECTIVE _____

PLURAL NOUN _____

COLOR _____

ADJECTIVE _____

NOUN _____

PLURAL NOUN _____

NUMBER _____

PLURAL NOUN _____

COLOR _____

ADJECTIVE _____

NOUN _____

PLURAL NOUN _____

VERB ENDING IN "ING" _____

NOUN _____

VERB _____

MAD LIBS

RUBY SLIPPERS

Dorothy's _____ slippers are one of the most _____
        COLOR   ADJECTIVE

pieces of film memorabilia of all time! Even though Dorothy's

_____ were silver in the book, they were changed to
PLURAL NOUN

_____ for the movie to take advantage of the _____
    COLOR   ADJECTIVE

new _____ technology. Many pairs of _____ were
        NOUN   PLURAL NOUN

made for the movie, and _____ pairs still exist today. If you save
                            NUMBER

your _____, you might be able to own a piece of history!
      PLURAL NOUN

The slippers were originally white and then dyed _____. To
                                                      COLOR

make the shoes _____, over 2,000 sequins were added to each
                  ADJECTIVE

_____! The _____ that Judy Garland wore most
    NOUN   PLURAL NOUN

during the _____ of the movie can be seen today at the
            VERB ENDING IN "ING"

Smithsonian _____ in Washington, DC. And no, don't ask to
                NOUN

_____ them on!
    VERB

MAD LIBS® is fun to play with friends, but you can also play it by yourself! To begin with, DO NOT look at the story on the page below. Fill in the blanks on this page with the words called for. Then, using the words you have selected, fill in the blank spaces in the story.

Now you've created your own hilarious MAD LIBS® game!

HOW TO BE A MUNCHKIN IN THREE EASY STEPS

ADJECTIVE _____

COLOR _____

PLURAL NOUN _____

ADJECTIVE _____

ADJECTIVE _____

ADJECTIVE _____

NUMBER _____

VERB _____

PART OF BODY (PLURAL) _____

VERB ENDING IN "ING" _____

ADJECTIVE _____

PLURAL NOUN _____

ARTICLE OF CLOTHING (PLURAL) _____

ADJECTIVE _____

PLURAL NOUN _____

PLURAL NOUN _____

HOW TO BE A MUNCHKIN
IN THREE EASY STEPS

The Munchkins are the _____ natives of Munchkinland who
ADJECTIVE

sing Dorothy off on her way to the _____ City. It may seem
COLOR

like fun and _____ to be a Munchkin, but it's actually
PLURAL NOUN

_____ work! If you're considering a permanent move to
ADJECTIVE

Munchkinland, here are some _____ things to know.
ADJECTIVE

1. You have to be really _____! If you're not under
ADJECTIVE

   _____ feet tall, be prepared to _____ on
   NUMBER   VERB

   your _____.
   PART OF BODY (PLURAL)

2. Practice your _____! Munchkins are
   VERB ENDING IN "ING"

   _____ singers with high-pitched voices, so if
   ADJECTIVE

   you want to succeed in Munchkinland, you're going to

   have to work on your _____.
   PLURAL NOUN

3. Wear colorful _____! The
   ARTICLE OF CLOTHING (PLURAL)

   brighter, the better. Bonus points for a/an _____
   ADJECTIVE

   hat and pointy _____.
   PLURAL NOUN

Once you've mastered these three _____, you're ready to
PLURAL NOUN

make your Munchkinland debut!

MAD LIBS® is fun to play with friends, but you can also play it by yourself! To begin with, DO NOT look at the story on the page below. Fill in the blanks on this page with the words called for. Then, using the words you have selected, fill in the blank spaces in the story.

Now you've created your own hilarious MAD LIBS® game!

THE DARK SIDE OF OZ

ADJECTIVE _____

ADJECTIVE _____

NOUN _____

PLURAL NOUN _____

COLOR _____

NOUN _____

VERB ENDING IN "ING" _____

LETTER OF THE ALPHABET _____

ADJECTIVE _____

ANIMAL _____

A PLACE _____

NOUN _____

VERB _____

COLOR _____

NOUN _____

PLURAL NOUN _____

ADJECTIVE _____

VERB _____

MAD LIBS®
THE DARK SIDE OF OZ

Even though *The Wizard of Oz* is a feel-_____ movie, there's a
ADJECTIVE

dark side to this classic. For one thing, there's a/an _____
ADJECTIVE

urban legend that you can see a Munchkin hanging from a/an

_____ in the background of a scene where Dorothy and her
NOUN

_____ skip down the _____ Brick Road singing
PLURAL NOUN   COLOR

"We're Off to See the _____." There is something
NOUN

_____ from the tree in the VH-_____
VERB ENDING IN "ING"   LETTER OF THE ALPHABET

version of the movie from the 1980s, but it's not a/an _____
ADJECTIVE

Munchkin. It's actually a/an _____ borrowed from (the)
ANIMAL

_____ Zoo! Another dark _____ to *The Wizard of*
A PLACE   NOUN

Oz is the rumor that if you _____ it while listening to the
VERB

_____ Floyd album *The Dark Side of the* _____, the
COLOR   NOUN

two _____ match up. Even though it wasn't intentional,
PLURAL NOUN

this rumor appears to be _____! Go ahead and _____
ADJECTIVE   VERB

it for yourself!

MAD LIBS® is fun to play with friends, but you can also play it by yourself! To begin with, DO NOT look at the story on the page below. Fill in the blanks on this page with the words called for. Then, using the words you have selected, fill in the blank spaces in the story.

Now you've created your own hilarious MAD LIBS® game!

FUN FACTS, PART ONE

NOUN _____

NUMBER _____

ADJECTIVE _____

NOUN _____

NOUN _____

PERSON IN ROOM (MALE) _____

LETTER OF THE ALPHABET _____

ADJECTIVE _____

ANIMAL _____

VERB _____

NOUN _____

NOUN _____

PLURAL NOUN _____

PLURAL NOUN _____

PERSON IN ROOM (FEMALE) _____

MAD LIBS®
FUN FACTS, PART ONE

You may have watched *The* _____ *of Oz* over _____
NOUN   NUMBER

times, but do you know these _____ facts about your favorite
ADJECTIVE

_____?
NOUN

- The name Oz comes from _____ files that
  NOUN

  L. _____ Baum was looking at labeled
  PERSON IN ROOM (MALE)

  A–_____ and *O–Z.*
  LETTER OF THE ALPHABET

- In the original script, Dorothy had a/an _____
  ADJECTIVE

  relationship with the human counterpart of the

  Scare-_____. It's why she says to him at the end,
  ANIMAL

  "I think I'll _____ you most of all."
  VERB

- There was a musical _____ called "The Jitterbug"
  NOUN

  that was cut for the final _____.
  NOUN

- The movie is 101 _____ long, but was originally
  PLURAL NOUN

  120 _____ long.
  PLURAL NOUN

- _____ Temple was first considered for
  PERSON IN ROOM (FEMALE)

  the role of Dorothy.

Published by Price Stern Sloan, an imprint of Penguin Group (USA), 345 Hudson Street, New York, NY 10014.

MAD LIBS® is fun to play with friends, but you can also play it by yourself! To begin with, DO NOT look at the story on the page below. Fill in the blanks on this page with the words called for. Then, using the words you have selected, fill in the blank spaces in the story.

Now you've created your own hilarious MAD LIBS® game!

ARE YOU A GOOD WITCH OR A BAD WITCH?

ADJECTIVE _____

NOUN _____

ANIMAL (PLURAL) _____

ADJECTIVE _____

ADJECTIVE _____

ARTICLE OF CLOTHING _____

ADJECTIVE _____

ADJECTIVE _____

COLOR _____

ADJECTIVE _____

PLURAL NOUN _____

ADJECTIVE _____

VERB _____

ADJECTIVE _____

COLOR _____

ADJECTIVE _____

MAD LIBS®
ARE YOU A GOOD WITCH OR A BAD WITCH?

There are two _____ witches in *The Wizard of Oz*. Pick a side!
ADJECTIVE

Which _____ do you like better?
NOUN

* You think winged _____ are totally
ANIMAL (PLURAL)

  _____ and not at all scary: You appreciate the
  ADJECTIVE

  _____ Witch of the West.
  ADJECTIVE

* You won't leave the house without your

  _____ and _____ crown and
  ARTICLE OF CLOTHING   ADJECTIVE

  tiara: You favor Glinda the _____ Witch.
  ADJECTIVE

* Your favorite color is emerald _____: You fancy
  COLOR

  the _____ Witch of the West.
  ADJECTIVE

* You travel around in giant floating _____:
  PLURAL NOUN

  Glinda the _____ Witch is more your style.
  ADJECTIVE

* You're afraid to _____ and won't go anywhere near
  VERB

  the water: You prefer the _____ Witch of the West.
  ADJECTIVE

* You know the power of the _____ slippers: Glinda
  COLOR

  the _____ Witch is right up your alley.
  ADJECTIVE

MAD LIBS® is fun to play with friends, but you can also play it by yourself! To begin with, DO NOT look at the story on the page below. Fill in the blanks on this page with the words called for. Then, using the words you have selected, fill in the blank spaces in the story.

Now you've created your own hilarious MAD LIBS® game!

THE TRUTH ABOUT TOTO

NOUN _____

ADJECTIVE _____

ANIMAL _____

PERSON IN ROOM (FEMALE) _____

PLURAL NOUN _____

VERB _____

PART OF THE BODY _____

NOUN _____

VERB ENDING IN "ING" _____

ANIMAL _____

NOUN _____

ADJECTIVE _____

ADVERB _____

NUMBER _____

NOUN _____

NOUN _____

A PLACE _____

MAD LIBS

THE TRUTH ABOUT TOTO

In *The* _____ *of Oz*, the most _____ character by far

NOUN · ADJECTIVE

is Toto, Dorothy's pet _____. In the movie, Toto was played

ANIMAL

by a female brindle cairn terrier named _____! She

PERSON IN ROOM (FEMALE)

was paid a salary of $125 each week. That was more _____

PLURAL NOUN

than any of the Munchkins made to _____ in the movie!

VERB

During filming, her _____ was broken when a/an

PART OF THE BODY

_____ accidentally stepped on it. While "Toto" was

NOUN

_____, an understudy _____ played her role.

VERB ENDING IN "ING" · ANIMAL

After the release of the _____, the dog became so

NOUN

_____ that her owners _____ changed her name to

ADJECTIVE · ADVERB

Toto! She starred in _____ films after *The* _____ *of Oz*.

NUMBER · NOUN

You can visit Toto's _____ in the Hollywood Forever Cemetery

NOUN

in (the) _____.

A PLACE

MAD LIBS® is fun to play with friends, but you can also play it by yourself! To begin with, DO NOT look at the story on the page below. Fill in the blanks on this page with the words called for. Then, using the words you have selected, fill in the blank spaces in the story.

Now you've created your own hilarious MAD LIBS® game!

WHICH CHARACTER ARE YOU?

PART OF THE BODY _____

PLURAL NOUN _____

NOUN _____

NOUN _____

VERB ENDING IN "ING" _____

PERSON IN ROOM _____

NOUN _____

PLURAL NOUN _____

NOUN _____

PLURAL NOUN _____

NOUN _____

ANIMAL _____

ADJECTIVE _____

ANIMAL _____

NOUN _____

Dorothy has three friends in Oz: the Tin Man, who wants a/an

_____; the Scarecrow, who wants a brain; and the Cowardly
<u>PART OF THE BODY</u>

Lion, who wants to be courageous. Which of Dorothy's

_____ are you most like?
<u>PLURAL NOUN</u>

1. You're hiding in the _____-room at school. What happened?
    <u>NOUN</u>

    a) You flunked your _____.
       <u>NOUN</u>

    b) You are _____ from a bully.
       <u>VERB ENDING IN "ING"</u>

    c) You are trying to avoid your crush, _____!
       <u>PERSON IN ROOM</u>

2. Your favorite after-__ _____ ____ activity is:
    <u>NOUN</u>

    a) reading a book about _____.
       <u>PLURAL NOUN</u>

    b) sitting locked in your _____, away from all the
       <u>NOUN</u>

       _____ that scare you.
       <u>PLURAL NOUN</u>

    c) doodling your _____'s name in your notebook.
       <u>NOUN</u>

If you picked *A*s, you're most like the Scare-_____. If you
                                                    <u>ANIMAL</u>

picked *B*s, you're _____ like the Cowardly _____.
                    <u>ADJECTIVE</u>   <u>ANIMAL</u>

And if you picked *C*s, you're a lot like the _____ Man.
                                              <u>NOUN</u>

MAD LIBS® is fun to play with friends, but you can also play it by yourself! To begin with, DO NOT look at the story on the page below. Fill in the blanks on this page with the words called for. Then, using the words you have selected, fill in the blank spaces in the story.

Now you've created your own hilarious MAD LIBS® game!

WHAT WOULD YOU WISH FOR?

NOUN _____

VERB ENDING IN "ING" _____

A PLACE _____

ADJECTIVE _____

ANIMAL _____

ADJECTIVE _____

NOUN _____

ADJECTIVE _____

NOUN _____

PART OF THE BODY _____

ANIMAL _____

NOUN _____

NOUN _____

PART OF THE BODY _____

ADVERB _____

NOUN _____

VERB _____

NOUN _____

MAD LIBS

WHAT WOULD YOU WISH FOR?

The _____ of Oz has the power to grant wishes to anyone
    NOUN

who comes _____ for help. Dorothy just wants to find a
    VERB ENDING IN "ING"

way to go home to (the) _____. If you were meeting the
    A PLACE

Wizard of Oz, what would you ask for? Would you want to be more

_____, like the Cowardly _____? If you were, you
    ADJECTIVE   ANIMAL

could try a/an _____ new trick on your _____-board
    ADJECTIVE   NOUN

or talk to that _____ new _____ across the street. Or
    ADJECTIVE   NOUN

maybe you'd rather wish for a/an _____, like the Scare-
    PART OF THE BODY

_____. That way, you'd never have trouble with your
    ANIMAL

_____ homework again! Or you might want to ask for a heart,
    NOUN

like the _____ Man. But chances are you already have a/an
    NOUN

_____! So maybe you'd rather have something _____
PART OF THE BODY   ADVERB

different, like a/an _____ to play Mad Libs with!
    NOUN

_____ carefully, because you only get one _____!
    VERB   NOUN

MAD LIBS® is fun to play with friends, but you can also play it by yourself! To begin with, DO NOT look at the story on the page below. Fill in the blanks on this page with the words called for. Then, using the words you have selected, fill in the blank spaces in the story.

Now you've created your own hilarious MAD LIBS® game!

FUN FACTS, PART TWO

ADJECTIVE _____

NOUN _____

ADJECTIVE _____

ADJECTIVE _____

PLURAL NOUN _____

PLURAL NOUN _____

COLOR _____

NOUN _____

ANIMAL (PLURAL) _____

ADJECTIVE _____

VERB _____

ADJECTIVE _____

PLURAL NOUN _____

ADJECTIVE _____

PART OF THE BODY (PLURAL) _____

COLOR _____

FUN FACTS, PART TWO

Here are more _____ facts about *The* _____ *of Oz*!
               ADJECTIVE   NOUN

Learn them all to become a/an _____ *Wizard of Oz* expert!
                                     ADJECTIVE

- The Munchkins were played by a/an _____
  ADJECTIVE

  vaudeville group from Europe called the Singer

  _____. Most of the _____ couldn't
    PLURAL NOUN   PLURAL NOUN

  even speak English!

- The _____ slippers in the Smithsonian
         COLOR

  _____ are mismatched.
    NOUN

- The multicolored _____ in the Emerald
                     ANIMAL (PLURAL)

  City were colored with _____ Jell-O crystals.
                    ADJECTIVE

- You can _____ the _____ Witch of the
          VERB   ADJECTIVE

  East outside Dorothy's window during the tornado scene.

  Most _____ think it's the _____ Witch
       PLURAL NOUN   ADJECTIVE

  of the West, but look at her _____. She's
                           PART OF THE BODY (PLURAL)

  wearing _____ slippers!
         COLOR

Published by Price Stern Sloan, an imprint of Penguin Group (USA), 345 Hudson Street, New York, NY 10014.

MAD LIBS® is fun to play with friends, but you can also play it by yourself! To begin with, DO NOT look at the story on the page below. Fill in the blanks on this page with the words called for. Then, using the words you have selected, fill in the blank spaces in the story.

Now you've created your own hilarious MAD LIBS® game!

FOLLOW THE RED BRICK ROAD

NOUN _____

NOUN _____

COLOR _____

COLOR _____

NOUN _____

ADJECTIVE _____

ADJECTIVE _____

ADJECTIVE _____

ADJECTIVE _____

NOUN _____

PLURAL NOUN _____

COLOR _____

NOUN _____

ADJECTIVE _____

EXCLAMATION _____

NOUN _____

ADJECTIVE _____

MAD LIBS®
FOLLOW THE RED BRICK ROAD

In *The* _____ *of Oz*, Dorothy is told to follow the Yellow

      NOUN

_____ Road to the _____ City. But intertwined with

  NOUN   COLOR

the _____ Brick Road is another _____—the Red

    COLOR   NOUN

Brick Road! Where does this mysterious, _____ road lead to?

                  ADJECTIVE

Here are a few _____ guesses:

        ADJECTIVE

- Directly to the _____ Witch of the West's castle.

        ADJECTIVE

  Hey, those _____ Winkies wanted a shortcut!

     ADJECTIVE

- Back to Dorothy's _____ in Kansas. She could

        NOUN

  have saved herself a lot of _____ if she had

        PLURAL NOUN

  taken the _____ Brick Road instead.

    COLOR

- Back to Munchkinland. Turns out, the Red Brick

  _____ wasn't a road at all—it just went around in

  NOUN

  a/an _____ circle. _____!

    ADJECTIVE   EXCLAMATION

- Behind the _____ of Oz's _____ curtain!

      NOUN   ADJECTIVE

MAD LIBS® is fun to play with friends, but you can also play it by yourself! To begin with, DO NOT look at the story on the page below. Fill in the blanks on this page with the words called for. Then, using the words you have selected, fill in the blank spaces in the story.

Now you've created your own hilarious MAD LIBS® game!

A WIZARD OF OZ COSTUME PARTY

ADJECTIVE _____

VERB _____

ADVERB _____

NOUN _____

VERB _____

PLURAL NOUN _____

COLOR _____

PLURAL NOUN _____

ADJECTIVE _____

PART OF THE BODY (PLURAL) _____

ANIMAL _____

NOUN _____

SILLY WORD _____

COLOR _____

NOUN _____

ADJECTIVE _____

PART OF THE BODY _____

A WIZARD OF OZ COSTUME PARTY

If you're looking for a/an _____ getup for your next costume
<u>ADJECTIVE</u>

party, _____ no further! The costumes from *The Wizard of*
<u>VERB</u>

Oz are _____ timeless, so why not dress as your favorite
<u>ADVERB</u>

_____? Here are instructions to help you _____ a
<u>NOUN</u>   <u>VERB</u>

costume that will impress all your _____. If you want to go
<u>PLURAL NOUN</u>

as **Dorothy**, grab a/an _____ dress. Paint your
<u>COLOR</u>

_____ red, and glue _____ sequins all over them.
<u>PLURAL NOUN</u>   <u>ADJECTIVE</u>

Wear your _____ in pigtails. Bonus points if you can
<u>PART OF THE BODY (PLURAL)</u>

find a/an _____ to bring with you! If you want to go as the
<u>ANIMAL</u>

Tin Man, wrap your entire body in _____-foil! Easy-
<u>NOUN</u>

_____! If you want to go as the **Scarecrow**, wear a/an
<u>SILLY WORD</u>

_____ sweat suit, and glue straw all over your _____.
<u>COLOR</u>   <u>NOUN</u>

And if you want to go as the **Cowardly Lion**, borrow your mom's

_____ fur coat, and paint your _____ to look like a
<u>ADJECTIVE</u>   <u>PART OF THE BODY</u>

lion. *Roar!*

MAD LIBS® is fun to play with friends, but you can also play it by yourself! To begin with, DO NOT look at the story on the page below. Fill in the blanks on this page with the words called for. Then, using the words you have selected, fill in the blank spaces in the story.

Now you've created your own hilarious MAD LIBS® game!

HOW TO BE COURAGEOUS, BY TOTO

NOUN _____

ANIMAL _____

ADJECTIVE _____

ADJECTIVE _____

PLURAL NOUN _____

PERSON IN ROOM (FEMALE) _____

ADJECTIVE _____

EXCLAMATION _____

ADJECTIVE _____

NOUN _____

NOUN _____

ADJECTIVE _____

PLURAL NOUN _____

SILLY WORD _____

ADJECTIVE _____

MAD LIBS®
HOW TO BE COURAGEOUS, BY TOTO

One of the most popular heroes of the movie *The* _____ *of Oz*
NOUN

is Toto, Dorothy's pet _____! Listen in on this never-before-
ANIMAL

heard conversation between the _____ Lion and Toto:
ADJECTIVE

Cowardly Lion: Toto, you're so _____! How did you get the
ADJECTIVE

_____   to   save   _____   from   the
PLURAL NOUN   PERSON IN ROOM (FEMALE)

_____ Witch of the West's castle?
ADJECTIVE

Toto: Bark! Bark! _____!
EXCLAMATION

Cowardly Lion: I see, I see. That's very _____. And what
ADJECTIVE

about when you pulled aside the _____ and revealed that the
NOUN

_____ of Oz was actually _____? Weren't you scared
NOUN   ADJECTIVE

of all the smoke and _____?
PLURAL NOUN

Toto: Bark! Bark! _____!
SILLY WORD

Cowardly Lion: Thanks for all the _____ help, Toto! Who
ADJECTIVE

needs the Wizard when I've got you?

MAD LIBS® is fun to play with friends, but you can also play it by yourself! To begin with, DO NOT look at the story on the page below. Fill in the blanks on this page with the words called for. Then, using the words you have selected, fill in the blank spaces in the story.

Now you've created your own hilarious MAD LIBS® game!

APPLES TO APPLES

NOUN _____

NOUN _____

TYPE OF FOOD (PLURAL) _____

ADJECTIVE _____

PERSON IN ROOM (FEMALE) _____

PLURAL NOUN _____

VERB _____

PERSON IN ROOM (FEMALE) _____

ADJECTIVE _____

NUMBER _____

NOUN _____

COLOR _____

TYPE OF LIQUID _____

COLOR _____

VERB ENDING IN "ING" _____

PLURAL NOUN _____

NUMBER _____

MAD LIBS
APPLES TO APPLES

Dorothy and the Scarecrow are walking through an apple

_____ when they are attacked by a/an _____
NOUN   NOUN

throwing _____! The tree is _____ and
          TYPE OF FOOD (PLURAL)   ADJECTIVE

doesn't want _____ to eat any of his apples. Too
              PERSON IN ROOM (FEMALE)

bad, because Dorothy could have used the _____
                                          PLURAL NOUN

to _____ Auntie _____'s _____
    VERB   PERSON IN ROOM (FEMALE)   ADJECTIVE

recipe for apple crisp!

Auntie Em's Apple Crisp

Slice _____ apples and place them in a/an _____.
      NUMBER   NOUN

Sprinkle with a mixture of _____ sugar, flour, and
                            COLOR

cinnamon. Cover with _____. Crumble a mixture of
                      TYPE OF LIQUID

oats, flour, _____ sugar, _____ soda, and
              COLOR   VERB ENDING IN "ING"

butter on top of the _____. Bake at _____ degrees
                      PLURAL NOUN   NUMBER

for 45 minutes and enjoy!

MAD LIBS® is fun to play with friends, but you can also play it by yourself! To begin with, DO NOT look at the story on the page below. Fill in the blanks on this page with the words called for. Then, using the words you have selected, fill in the blank spaces in the story.

Now you've created your own hilarious MAD LIBS® game!

THERE'S NO PLACE LIKE HOME

NOUN _____

ADJECTIVE _____

ADJECTIVE _____

PERSON IN ROOM (FEMALE) _____

VERB _____

EXCLAMATION _____

ADJECTIVE _____

COLOR _____

NOUN _____

ADJECTIVE _____

ADJECTIVE _____

VERB _____

NOUN _____

ADJECTIVE _____

NUMBER _____

PERSON IN ROOM (FEMALE) _____

ADJECTIVE _____

ADJECTIVE _____

At the end of *The Wizard of Oz*, Dorothy wakes up in her _____
NOUN

in Kansas and realizes that her visit to the Land of Oz was all just a/an

_____ dream! She's so _____ to be home that she
ADJECTIVE   ADJECTIVE

promises Auntie _____ that she's never going to
PERSON IN ROOM (FEMALE)

_____ again. _____—no wonder she doesn't want to
VERB   EXCLAMATION

leave Kansas! Dorothy had to fight the _____ Witch of the
ADJECTIVE

West on her way to the _____ City to meet the _____
COLOR   NOUN

of Oz in hopes that he would grant her _____ wish to go
ADJECTIVE

home. But when she got there, the Wizard of Oz turned out to be a big,

_____ fraud! He promised to _____ her, and then
ADJECTIVE   VERB

floated away in a hot-air _____! Luckily, Glinda the
NOUN

_____ Witch was there to tell Dorothy to click her heels
ADJECTIVE

_____ times. Even though Auntie _____ says it
NUMBER   PERSON IN ROOM (FEMALE)

was all a/an _____ dream, it's better to be _____
ADJECTIVE   ADJECTIVE

than sorry!

Published by Price Stern Sloan, an imprint of Penguin Group (USA), 345 Hudson Street, New York, NY 10014.

This book is published by

PSS!
PRICE STERN SLOAN

whose other splendid titles include
such literary classics as